Heartfelt Goodbye

How to Write and Deliver the Eulogy Your Loved
One Deserves

Bruce Rule

Acknowledgments

I am eternally grateful to Caitlin Harpin for the editing and feedback that greatly improved this book; Carmina Mevs for keeping the project on track through her encouragement; and the members of the Clark Writer's Workshop for their support.

A special "thank you" goes to my wife, Pamela Rule, who proofread this book for phrasing and grammar mistakes.

Dedicated to the memory of

Mary F. "Bunny" Rule

1932-2021

Contents

How to Use This Book

If you have been chosen to give a eulogy, let me first say I am sorry for your loss. I did not know your loved one, but I know this must be a difficult time for you. Not only are you grieving, you may feel a heavy weight for having taken on the responsibility of writing and delivering the eulogy.

While this is a difficult time, look at a eulogy as an opportunity to pay tribute to your loved one, an occasion for you and those close to you to deal with the grief together.

Keep in mind that you are not being asked to detail your loved one's entire life in a eulogy. Nor should you feel the need to include any negative events or to justify what the person did while alive.

Instead, you should see the eulogy as an opportunity to share what made your loved one special. This is a time when you can speak from your heart and remind those who have gathered about your loved one's unique qualities, and why he or she will be missed.

A loved one's death can spur a wide variety of emotions. Grief and sadness, of course, but some people just go numb. Others may feel anger at the unjustness of the world, while some feel relief that the loved one's suffering is over.

While it's impossible for me to know exactly how you feel at this moment, I can tell you that I have been in your situation.

My mother, Mary "Bunny" Rule, passed away in October 2021. I felt it was my duty to give her a proper eulogy at the memorial service that we held (a memorial service that she had planned in a letter she entrusted to me years earlier). Because my father had died when I was a little child, my mother was the only parent I really knew. She was very special to me.

She was also very special to a lot of other people because of her big heart, her outgoing personality and her love for others. Even though she wasn't famous and she won't ever be profiled in a history book, she deserved a proper and heartfelt farewell.

Writing a eulogy that explained how special my mother was while coping with my grief turned out to be difficult. It was hard even though I am a journalist with decades of writing experience, as well as an award-winning public speaker.

As I worked through what I wanted to say about her I came to realize that the process of putting together a eulogy was helping me deal with my grief. I also came to realize that sharing what I felt would help me deal with my loss.

I began to see the eulogy as a way for those who gathered at her memorial service to share our love and our grief in a way that would be healing.

In the following chapters I will walk you through the process of putting together and writing a fitting eulogy for your loved one.

I will show you how I put together my mother's eulogy in exact detail so you can use it as a guide for yours. As painful as it was to write and deliver the speech, I can assure you that it helped with my grieving.

I will also provide guidance on how to prepare for delivering the eulogy, both on the day of the service and beforehand. If at any point during the process you feel you need more help you can reach out to me at rulecommunications.com.

I know that you are still working through many emotions dealing with the loss of your loved one.

Rest assured if you use the techniques in the following chapters you will be able to write and deliver the eulogy your loved one deserves.

CHAPTER ONE

Preparing to Write a Eulogy

Most eulogies are given at the funeral or memorial service, and these tend to be within days of a person's death. Because time may be short, you should put a high priority on setting the time aside to prepare, write and practice the eulogy. Everyone is different, so it is hard to know how much time you will need.

You will want to take your time and give the eulogy your undivided attention. While I can't say exactly how long you will need, I can say that as an experienced writer and public speaker it took me more than six hours, over several days, to prepare, write and practice my mother's eulogy.

Many times the person giving the eulogy may also be asked to help with funeral arrangements, offering solace to the grieving, writing and placing the obituary and other tasks that come up in the wake of a person's passing. Try to pass off as many of these tasks to friends and family as you can. Also ask a friend or family member to help with the daily household chores that you normally do. It's really important that you have the time and quiet space to concentrate on the eulogy.

The first thing I would like you to do is find a spot where you can sit undisturbed while you work on the eulogy. It would be hard for you to concentrate if you try to do this, say, at your kitchen table with people walking in and out or on the subway while you commute back and forth to work. You need a quiet spot to reflect on your loved one and your times together.

Plan on setting aside a good hour or two for this first step. It may take you less time, but the important thing is to give yourself enough time so you don't feel rushed.

You will need paper and something to write with. If you are more comfortable with using a computer, do that. The important part is that you are able to record your thoughts. Don't try to do all of the following in your mind alone.

Sit down, take a deep breath and try to relax for a few moments. Clear your mind of everything so you can collect your thoughts of your loved one.

Now, what comes to mind when you think of your loved one?

What adjectives do you associate with your loved one? Was she quiet? Loud? Generous? Outgoing? Shy? Write down four or five adjectives or phrases that you or others would use to describe your loved one.

How did your loved one spend her days? Was she always helping out in the community? Was he the one who always had the right tool in the garage for any job? Was she a great singer? Was he known for speaking several languages? Write down a few of the things that pop to mind.

Now write down anything else that comes to mind when you think of your loved one. For instance:

- Memories of big events and small moments.
- Silly things that happened as well as quiet ones.
- Phrases that they used.

- Achievements, hobbies, favorite movies and poems.
- Physical attributes that everyone noticed.
- Anything unique about their home or car.
- Stayed in one place for decades, or moved a lot.
- Jobs they had or work they did.
- Different languages they spoke, skills they had.
- Unique things that they owned or did.

Write everything down. There is no need to edit right now. You are simply brainstorming. Just get everything down on paper, and don't worry about misspellings, correct dates or the writing. Just put down a few words for each to spark your memory.

The things that are coming to mind easily for you are probably also the things that your family and friends are going to remember about your loved one.

If you are having trouble thinking clearly at this time, it is certainly fine to call, email or text family members and friends and invite them to share their thoughts.

Don't feel that you have to do this all alone, but also don't feel you have to include everything anybody tells you.

If someone's memory is different than yours, well, that can happen. There is no reason to argue. This is no time to get into a back-and-forth with anyone. Just make a note of it. If you decide you want to include something in the eulogy that is in dispute, you can take time later to determine the facts. And if the facts can't be determined, you can always mention this in the eulogy.

This process of writing down your memories almost certainly will be painful, of course. You are still grieving.

Once you have a good number of memories down on the page (or on your computer screen), step away for a bit. I can almost guarantee you will need a bit of time to calm your emotions.

When you feel you are able to, look over the list. Is there a common theme? Do your memories revolve around her volunteer work? Or his attempts at singing in public? Or an absolute dedication to whatever the family needed? Or how funny she was? How clumsy he could be?

When I gathered my memories about my mother, here are some of the things that came to my mind:

- Widow at age 36.

- Couldn't go to college because her father abandoned the family.

- Positive outlook – never complained. Laughed a lot.

- Couldn't put anything over on her – she always knew when someone was lying or shading the truth. At least she always caught me.

- Loved being around people. Family picnics all the time.

- Loved hearing and telling good stories.

- Seemed to be able to do just about anything athletic – called best basketball player in New Brunswick, New Jersey, male or female. Tall for a woman at six feet two inches.

- She wished she had been born in a more recent age when there were more opportunities for women. Believed she could have played in the WNBA.

- Raised two unruly children alone.
- Played semi-pro basketball and softball – not pro. Had to quit when she got married.
- Blue-collar jobs – security guard, bartender, ice cream factory (Mr. Smiley).
- Terrible with housework. Said if she had been born in a more liberated time she would have had a husband who stayed home while she went to work.
- Terrible cook – served a lot of pork roll and eggs. Burned everything.
- Overcame lots of health problems in her life.
- Liked gambling and poker and usually won.
- Made friends everywhere she went. Felt totally at ease talking to perfect strangers.

As you can see, my thoughts were pretty scattershot. Yours will be also, and that is OK.

Some of my thoughts focused on the sad times in her life. She had to give up a college scholarship to take a job to help support the family after her father abandoned them; she became a widow at age 36 after my father died; and she might have been able to be a pro athlete if she had been born just a few decades later.

Some of the memories are happy. She laughed a lot; she was an engaging storyteller; and she really enjoyed gambling and playing poker.

And some are just funny – she was a *really* bad cook.

Looking over my list a few common themes were apparent to me. She was a great competitor who usually won; she had a number of bad breaks in her life; and she had a positive attitude almost all the time.

When you feel you are able to, look over the list you brainstormed about your loved one.

Pick two or three themes that came to your mind when you thought of your loved one.

Don't worry if they seem contradictory or have nothing in common. That's natural. Your loved one, like everyone including you and me, was a complex human being, and we all have contradictions and inconsistencies.

It's what makes us human. It's what makes us real.

Remember that you shouldn't feel that you have to explain everything there was to know about your loved one. There is just so much you can say in one speech. While there is no set limit on how long a eulogy should be, you will want to focus only on the common themes.

As a rough guide, the eulogy I wrote for my mother was just over 1,600 words, or about five pages. Yours can be shorter. If you feel you need to say more, then go ahead. My advice is to try to keep it as short and to the point as you can.

Most people in attendance will have known your loved one on some level and have their own history with her. They will have their own understanding of who she was. They are there grieving for the person they knew, and their relationship might be different from yours.

Focus on what your thoughts of the loved one are, what you remember most, and how you see her. Doing so is the best way for your love to shine through. It will be *your* tribute to her.

If you are honest while expressing your feelings, your audience will understand and appreciate what you are saying. Your words will be a great comfort to them because they will recognize the person you are describing. You will be sharing your truth as well as theirs.

This will be true even if you feel you must discuss your loved one's flaws or failings, as long as you are speaking from your heart and a position of love.

Let me give you an example of what I mean. A few years ago, my friend's father died. He was a good man and provider who took care of his family.

But what was one of the things that stood out about him for many of us? He told the most excruciatingly detailed, boring stories. All the time.

At his funeral, the only person who spoke was the family minister.

We were all lost in our own thoughts, remembering him while she spoke. She explained that when she asked his widow and children what they remembered about him, they all mentioned his way of putting people to sleep with his stories.

At that moment, those of us who had gathered felt a great release of emotions. We glanced at each other, taking great comfort in knowing that we all shared similar memories of him. It brought us together in that moment, and helped us with our grief.

However, do keep in mind that this is a tribute to the departed and it should give comfort to those gathered. Any mention of flaws or failings should be shared only with love. A eulogy is no place to settle a grudge or focus on anything negative about the departed.

After reviewing your list and finding the common themes you might want to take another break to get your emotions under control.

Now comes the part that you may find hardest, mainly because you may feel overwhelmed when trying to choose the words you will use when writing the eulogy.

You may be concerned that your words will seem inadequate, that they aren't expressing your thoughts perfectly or that they aren't good enough.

Try not to worry about any of that. The truth is the words you choose won't be as important as the feelings you convey and the memories that you share.

Speak honestly, speak from the heart. Your truth will be what matters the most. Don't feel you have to make profound statements about life or humanity or, really, anything.

You are simply there to focus on the life of your loved one.

Most likely, the people in attendance won't remember your exact words anyway. They will remember sharing in your grief and feeling comfort in knowing that you felt the same way about the departed one as they do.

To paraphrase poet Maya Angelou, people may not remember your words, but they will remember how your words made them feel.

As you will see when you read my mother's eulogy, I didn't use fancy words or worry about sentence structure. Sometimes I didn't even use full sentences, or explain things completely. When you speak from the heart no one will notice those things.

CHAPTER TWO

Writing Out What You Want to Say

Now that you have written down your memories and thoughts, it is time to organize them in a way that will best convey what you want.

The easiest way to organize your thoughts is one that is simple and effective. The following structure has been attributed to a lot of people dating back to Aristotle, and it is effective because it works. Here it is:

1) Tell them what you are going to tell them

2) Tell them

3) Tell them what you have told them

If that advice feels familiar it's because the structure is used by many public speakers to great effect.

Do not worry that you will sound repetitive. Remember, this eulogy will be about your loved one and how you feel. No one listening will be judging you. The people who are listening will relate what you are saying to their own thoughts and emotions about the departed, and the sameness will be a comfort to them.

Let's look at an example of how the structure can be used to honor someone who has passed away. In this example, the deceased is a woman who was the strength of the family, the one whom everyone relied on to get things done

Keeping the structure we outlined above in mind, the example eulogy could go something like this:

1) "We all know whom we could depend on when things got tough. We knew she would always be there." (*Tell them what you are going to tell them*).

2) Memories of how she helped others when there was trouble. One or more examples. (*Tell them.*)

3) "We will miss her coming in and helping whenever we needed her. But in the future, when times are tough, I am going to lean on her memory to get me through. Because for me she will always be there." (*Tell them what you told them.*)

Do you see how it works?

A real-life example of this structure is the eulogy that Billy Crystal gave for comedian Robin Williams at the Emmy Awards a number of years ago. The full speech can be found online.

Here is how Crystal used the structure to honor his departed friend:

1) Crystal started by saying Williams "made us laugh. Hard."

2) He then gave examples of Robin Williams being funny at a baseball game. At family functions, and on stage.

3) Crystal ended the eulogy by saying that people like Williams who make us laugh will shine forever, and warm our hearts forever.

While you can put your memories and stories in whatever order you think works best, in many ways it is easiest to just put them in chronological order. You don't have to strict about it. It may be easier for you to group the memories by subject matter, for instance.

When you read the eulogy that I wrote for my mother, you will see I jumped around a bit when talking about her life but in general kept things pretty much in chronological order.

When I sat down to write my mother's eulogy, I wanted people to understand just how amazing it was that she was a strong woman with a fun and positive attitude who was able to do some amazing things despite all the setbacks she endured. She loved life.

And looking over the memories I jotted down, I saw that the examples that illustrated my feelings mainly involved her athletic accomplishments.

Following is the eulogy I gave at her memorial service. Notice the structure: I talked about how strong she was, used some examples about what she accomplished, and ended by talking about the fact that her strength led me to believe that she would live through her illness.

In the next chapter we will go over this eulogy in more detail. I will explain how and why I chose what I included in my mother's eulogy to help you decide what to include in the eulogy you write.

Mary F. "Bunny" (Meyers) Rule 1932-2021

We've heard people talk today about how my mother was kind and funny and a great storyteller. And it's right that we remember those things about her.

But when I think of her the word that comes to my mind is strong.

We all know that she had a tough life. She was a star in high school, both academically and as an athlete. But she wasn't able to go to college. Instead, she had to go to work to support the family. Then she got married and ended up a widow at age 36, with two kids who were challenging in very different ways.

But she never complained about any of the hardships or about raising us alone. She just carried on.

In fact, I can only remember once her ever talking about being a single mother. It was back when I was in elementary school. I didn't much like school, and it didn't like me. I got into a lot of trouble, and Vice Principal Paladino used to call her in to explain what I did wrong and what my punishment was going to be.

And finally one day she said to him, "I don't need to come in here. If you say he did something, I believe you. Give him whatever punishment you think he deserves. Maybe you'll have better luck with him than I do. But, whatever you do, please don't suspend him. I'm a single mother who works nights and I need to sleep during the day."

When we left the office, I said to her, "Mom, you are supposed to be in there defending me!"

And that's when she gave me the look. You know the look I'm talking about…

When I was young all I heard was that she was the best basketball player in New Brunswick, male or female. The boys at the playground would run away when they saw her coming. I would roll my eyes and say, "Yeah, sure."

In high school, a new kid showed up in class. (My friend Mike. Some of you may remember him. He couldn't be here today). He told me that his parents had just gotten divorced so they moved back to this area because his Mom had grown up in New Brunswick, in the Sixth Ward. I said, so did my mother. I told him to see if his mother remembered Bunny Meyers.

And I went home that day and asked Mom if she remembered a Doreen Frank who grew up in the Sixth Ward. She said she didn't know Doreen directly, but she knew her older brothers, the Frank boys. They had been minor celebrities in the neighborhood because they had appeared as extras in a Broadway show.

That Monday, I told Mike what my mother said. He told me that his mother said she had been too young to remember my mother. Then he said his uncles were over on Sunday for dinner, so he asked them if they remembered Bunny Meyers.

He said their eyes flew open wide and they told him she was the best basketball player they ever saw. They said she would get mad at them because they would be playing basketball at the playground and when they saw her coming they would all remember they had to go do their homework. Mike said his uncles were laughing because they used to climb the fence at the back of the playground to get away while she was running up shaking her fist and calling out, "Come back, you cowards."

I said to Mike, "Really?"

He shrugged. "That's what they said."

I went home that afternoon and I told her, "I'm sorry." She said, "For what?"

I explained what Mike told me, and then I said, "I guess you <u>were</u> the best basketball player in New Brunswick."

That's when she gave me that look. Again.

After high school she played semi-pro basketball and softball for 10 years. She told her grandsons those were some of the happiest times of her life. Women athletes really didn't make any money back then, but she got to travel all around the Northeast, and they got uniforms and their meals taken care of.

She had to stop doing that after she got married, because married women weren't allowed to do stuff like that back then.

So she took up bowling. The first year in the league, she was the second-highest scorer. The next year she took over the top spot and held it for about 14 years until she stopped going.

If you remember, back in the kitchen of 610 Myrtle Road we always had a lot of those milk-white glasses with bowling figures on them. I just assumed she bought them somewhere, maybe as a lot at a garage sale. She later told me, no. The league gave out those glasses every time you bowled a game over 200. We had so many of those glasses she finally told them, "You know, forget it. I don't want anymore. Give them to somebody else."

Let me tell you how good she was. She was always getting called to be a substitute in the men's league. Which she liked because as a substitute you bowled for free. She said they called her so often she could have bowled for free six days a week. Some of the men got resentful because of how good she was, so they passed a rule that said only men could be substitutes in the men's league. They changed the rules to exclude her. That's how good she was.

I once asked her if she ever played golf, because my father played golf. She said he took her golfing once, to Tara Greens over on Route 27. He took her to the driving range, where they practiced for a while. He took her to the putting green and showed her how to putt. Then he took her to the par-3 course, because he said that would be easier for her to start with.

He pointed at the flag and said she should try to get the ball in the hole in three shots. The first shot she took landed right at the edge of the green. The second shot ended up a few inches from the hole. The third shot, right into the cup.

She said, "I handed him the club and told him, 'This is too easy. It's boring' and walked off the course. He never took me again."

Now you may not believe that story. But after what happened to me with the basketball, you know I believe it!

It's because she was able to do all this that it was such a shock to me when she died.

It shouldn't have been. Because she was 89, and she had inoperable lung cancer, and a blood infection in her feet that led to her losing some of her toes. She had fallen down, and broken her leg. And when they took her to the hospital they confirmed she had Covid on top of everything else.

That would have been enough to kill anybody. But whenever I talked to the doctors, all they were concerned about was the broken leg. How they set it and how they were hoping it would heal so she wouldn't need an operation. What rehab center I wanted her to go to. They even asked for permission for her to be included in a two-year study of how Covid affects cancer patients.

She was moved to the rehab center, and we talked the next morning. She said she was very tired. I told her to get some rest and that we would talk when she felt better. We would find out what the visitation rules were and I would visit when I was allowed.

That night at about 9 o'clock the rehab center called, and my first thought was I bet she forgot her phone charger or something and that's why she's having the nurse call.

When the rehab supervisor told me she died I was shocked. I just thought she would bull her way through this like she had done everything else in her life.

The supervisor told me that the nurse had checked on my mother at 6 o'clock, and that Mom had been tired but she was chatty and seemed to be in good spirits. Her old self. When they did a bed check at 8 o'clock, she was gone. She had died peacefully in her sleep.

I thought, at least she got that. She deserved a peaceful death after the troubles she had in her life. At least God gave her that.

Since her death I thought a lot about what Heaven must be like for her. And you <u>know</u> she is in Heaven. She always said that growing up on Morrell Street in the 1930s was heaven for kids, because they had the Rutgers campus right there, and Buccleuch Park, and the river to swim in.

But I think that heaven for her looks a lot like the side yard of 610 Myrtle Road back in the 1970s, when we used to have those big family picnics with everybody there. Billy Ricker and Joey Meyers swapping tall tales, Big Danny McCarthy and Arlene joining right in, Pauline's crazy giggle, the much-missed David Soden and so many of the others who are gone whose names I can't think of at this moment. And you know she's right in the middle of everything, laughing and joking as we speak.

I want to leave you with some words she wrote in that letter to me about her funeral arrangements.

"Remember me once in a while. The good things, of course. I wish you all a good life. May you be loved as I loved you all."

Now turn to the next chapter where we will go over my mother's eulogy in detail.

CHAPTER THREE

How I Put Together My Mother's Eulogy

Now that you have read the eulogy as a whole in the previous chapter, let's look at it in a more detailed manner.

"We've heard people talk today about how my mother was kind and funny and a great storyteller. And it's right that we remember those things about her.

But when I think of her the word that comes to my mind is strong."

Notice that I got right to the point I wanted to make: she was a strong person.

Being so direct was my way of following the structure we examined in the previous chapter: tell them what you are going to tell them.

I wasn't the first speaker at my mother's service. As I listened to the earlier speakers, I decided to acknowledge what they said in my introductory sentence by starting with "We've heard people talk today..." I had planned on saying that she was kind and a lot of fun. I ended up making a very small change to the first sentence, and it helped create a smooth transition between the previous eulogies and mine.

But note: do not feel that you must acknowledge what the other speakers have said. If you want to, that's fine. However, you may feel you have to tune out the other speakers to concentrate on what you are about to say. That's also fine.

Notice I mention right away that we are paying tribute to my mother. When you speak, it may be unclear to some of those at the service how you know the departed and what your relationship was. It would be a good idea to work that in at the beginning. You can even say straight out, "For anybody who doesn't know me…" and then explain your relationship with the departed.

Also notice that I didn't start out with a cliché like "We are gathered here today," or a standard greeting like "Hello" or "Good morning." I would suggest you skip those and go straight into what you want to say.

"We all know that she had a tough life. She was a star in high school, both academically and as an athlete. But she wasn't able to go to college. Instead, she had to go to work to support the family. Then she got married and ended up a widow at age 36, with two kids who were challenging in very different ways."

Most people at the service knew all this, so I didn't want to dwell on the obstacles she faced. It would have been too maudlin, and I felt that it wouldn't have been what she wanted. However, I thought it was important to point out the obstacles in a general way so people would understand just how strong she was.

By the way, the phrase, *"two kids who were challenging in very different ways,"* got a number of people in the audience smiling and nodding their heads. My older sibling and I were a handful, and everyone in the family knew it.

It also was enough of an explanation that those in attendance who did not know us when we were young would understand.

Although it is not required in a eulogy, it is almost always a good idea to mention the departed's family somewhere. It is especially important if you are not a family member.

"But she never complained about any of the hardships or about raising us alone. She just carried on.

In fact, I can only remember once her ever talking about being a single mother. It was back when I was in elementary school. I didn't much like school, and it didn't like me. I got into a lot of trouble, and Vice Principal Paladino used to call her in to explain what I did wrong and what my punishment was going to be.

And finally one day she said to him, "I don't need to come in here. If you say he did something, I believe you. Give him whatever punishment you think he deserves. Maybe you'll have better luck with him than I do. But, whatever you do, please don't suspend him. I'm a single mother who works nights and I need to sleep during the day."

My mother loved to tell stories, so I thought the best way to convey her "never complain" attitude was to tell this anecdote from my childhood. It was such a minor incident in the overall scheme of things that it emphasized how little she talked about the bad things that happened to her.

This really was the one time I do recall her ever calling attention to being a single mother, which is why it stood out in my memory. After the service, in fact, a number of people told me that this was the first time they had ever heard the story, and that they had never heard her complain either.

"When we left the office, I said to her, "Mom, you are supposed to be in there defending me!"

Do I remember the exact words? No, of course not. After all, we are talking about something that happened more than 50 years ago. But that is OK. It is perfectly fine if you want to tell a story like this one and don't get the exact words correct - as long as you aren't putting offensive or controversial comments into other people's mouths.

Try to get the meaning and feeling right, and people will understand if the words aren't exact.

"And that's when she gave me the look. You know the look I'm talking about..."

My mother had a signature look she would make when she knew you were trying to put something over on her. It was a knowing smile that said, "You aren't fooling me one bit." Mentioning that look gave everybody in the audience something to nod their heads about, because they could see it in their mind's eye. It was a way to bring a familiar comfort to them in their grief.

"When I was young all I heard was that she was the best basketball player in New Brunswick, male or female. The boys at the playground would run away when they saw her coming. I would roll my eyes and say, "Yeah, sure."

In high school, a new kid showed up in class. (My friend Mike. Some of you may remember him. He couldn't be here today). He told me that his parents had just gotten divorced so they moved back to this area because his Mom had grown up in New Brunswick, in the Sixth Ward. I said, so did my mother. I told him to see if his mother remembered Bunny Meyers.

And I went home that day and asked Mom if she remembered a Doreen Frank who grew up in the Sixth Ward. She said she didn't know Doreen directly, but she knew her older brothers, the Frank boys. They had been minor celebrities in the neighborhood because they had appeared as extras in a Broadway show.

That Monday, I told Mike what my mother said. He told me that his mother said she had been too young to remember my mother. Then he said his uncles were over on Sunday for dinner, so he asked them if they remembered Bunny Meyers.

He said their eyes flew open wide and they told him she was the best basketball player they ever saw. They said she would get mad at them because they would be playing basketball at the playground and when they saw her coming they would all remember they had to go do their homework. Mike said his uncles were laughing because they used to climb the fence at the back of the playground to get away while she was running up shaking her fist and calling out, "Come back, you cowards."

I said to Mike, "Really?"

He shrugged. "That's what they said."

I went home that afternoon and I told her, "I'm sorry." She said, "For what?"

I explained what Mike told me, and then I said, "I guess you were the best basketball player in New Brunswick."

That's when she gave me that look. Again."

I chose to talk about her basketball reputation at this point for a few reasons. The first was that she was extremely tall for a woman of her time (6'2") and looked like a basketball player. The second was that everyone who knew her had either known or heard that she had been a star basketball player.

It was a memory that we all shared.

I could have just said that she was the best basketball player in New Brunswick when she was young and left it at that. However, it's important in a eulogy to share your relationship with the loved one, to let people see how the two of you interacted. This story illustrates that very well, with me getting "that look" once again.

I also felt that this story was a better way to illustrate that everyone saw her as the best basketball player without listing a bunch of dry sports statistics. Whenever possible, when talking about your loved one, remember that you are sharing what you felt and understood. You don't need to add a bunch of dry facts to back up what you are saying. You can do so if you think it best conveys what you want to say, but don't feel you have to.

"After high school she played semi-pro basketball and softball for 10 years. She told her grandsons those were some of the happiest times of her life. Women athletes really didn't make any money back then, but she got to travel all around the Northeast, and they got uniforms and their meals taken care of.

She had to stop doing that after she got married, because married women weren't allowed to do stuff like that back then.

So she took up bowling. The first year in the league, she was the second-highest scorer. The next year she took over the top spot and held it for about 14 years until she stopped going.

If you remember, back in the kitchen of 610 Myrtle Road we always had a lot of those milk-white glasses with bowling figures on them. I just assumed she bought them somewhere, maybe as a lot at a garage sale. She later told me, no. The league gave out those glasses every time you bowled a game over 200. We had so many of those glasses she finally told them, "You know, forget it. I don't want anymore. Give them to somebody else."

Let me tell you how good she was. She was always getting called to be a substitute in the men's league. Which she liked because as a substitute you bowled for free. She said they called her so often she could have bowled for free six days a week. Some of the men got resentful because of how good she was, so they passed a rule that said only men could be substitutes in the men's league. They changed the rules to exclude her. That's how good she was."

Here I relate some of her other athletic accomplishments. While I mentioned that she never made much money playing semi-pro and she was forced to quit after she got married, but notice that I didn't focus or dwell on those setbacks. Instead, I used that to emphasize her positive attitude – she couldn't play semi-pro ball, so she picked up bowling and became very good at that instead.

If you are wondering about how detailed your story should be, keep in mind that you are sharing memories of your loved one that are bringing comfort to the people who have gathered with you. For anyone who spent any time at all in the kitchen of 610 Myrtle Road my mention of those glasses brought back a comforting shared memory of friends and family hanging out in our home.

Was there some object that everyone associated with your loved one? Did she always wear a baseball cap when she left the house? Did he have a Notre Dame tattoo? The latest sports car, or an old jalopy? These personal things about your loved one may sound small, but if you mention them in your eulogy they will bring comfort to those who remember them.

"I once asked her if she ever played golf, because my father played golf. She said he took her golfing once, to Tara Greens over on Route 27. He took her to the driving range, where they practiced for a while. He took her to the putting green and showed her how to putt. Then he took her to the Par-3 course, because he said that would be easier for her to start with.

He pointed at the flag and said she should try to get the ball in the hole in three shots. The first shot she took landed right at the edge of the green. The second shot ended up a few inches from the hole. The third shot, right into the cup.

She said, "I handed him the club and told him, 'This is too easy. It's boring' and walked off the course. He never took me again."

Here is one more story about her amazing accomplishments. It also sounds the most unlikely. By telling the other stories first I had already made it clear that she was a great athlete who really could do amazing things. If this story wasn't true, well, it could have been.

The question you may have: do I know if it is true? No, I don't. My father died many years ago and as far as I know he never mentioned this story to anyone. Does it matter if my mother was 100% truthful when she told it to me? No, it does not.

Why? Because she was a person who loved telling stories, and everyone who knew her could easily imagine her telling this one to me, whether it was exaggerated or not.

"Now you may not believe that story. But after what happened to me with the basketball, you know I believe it!"

And here I acknowledge the story is unbelievable. Then I point out that I had been proven wrong when I doubted that she was the best basketball player in New Brunswick and later found out that it was true, so I'm going to believe this one anyway.

By bringing the eulogy back to the basketball story, I have tied up what I wanted to say about her sports accomplishments.

"It's because she was able to do all this that it was such a shock to me when she died."

This sentence is a signal that we are moving on from the amazing things she accomplished to discuss her death.

"It shouldn't have been. Because she was 89, and she had inoperable lung cancer, and a blood infection in her feet that led to her losing some of her toes. She had fallen down, and broken her leg. And when they took her to the hospital they confirmed she had Covid on top of everything else.

That would have been enough to kill anybody. But whenever I talked to the doctors, all they were concerned about was the broken leg. How they set it and how they were hoping it would heal so she wouldn't need an operation. What rehab center I wanted her to go to. They even asked for permission for her to be included in a two-year study of how Covid affects cancer patients.

She was moved to the rehab center, and we talked the next morning. She said she was very tired. I told her to get some rest and that we would talk when she felt better. We would find out what the visitation rules were and I would visit when I was allowed.

That night about 9 o'clock the rehab center called, and my first thought was I bet she forgot her phone charger or something and that's why she's having the nurse call.

When the rehab supervisor told me she died, I was shocked. I just thought she would bull her way through this like she had done everything else in her life."

Some people advise that you should never talk about the cause of death. I say, talk about it if you have a reason to do so. But don't feel you have to go into any details if you don't think it would be fitting, or if your loved one would not have wanted the information to be shared.

I felt the need to explain the circumstances of her death because people had been asking and I hadn't gotten around to telling anyone what happened. I don't think that my mother would have minded.

However, notice that I emphasized the fact that I was shocked because I was so used to her overcoming setbacks and carrying on. I had come to depend so much on her strength that I couldn't believe she had died. I think that is what many family members and friends felt as well, so sharing how I felt was a comfort to them.

"The supervisor told me that the nurse had checked on my mother at 6 o'clock, and that Mom had been tired but she was chatty and seemed to be in good spirits. Her old self. When they did a bed check at 8 o'clock, she was gone. She had died peacefully in her sleep.

I thought, at least she got that. She deserved a peaceful death after the troubles she had in her life. At least God gave her that."

I mentioned that she was chatty and in good spirits even after being so sick to emphasize her positive attitude toward life. I also think it was comforting to know that she died peacefully without a long struggle.

"Since her death I thought a lot about what Heaven must be like for her. And you <u>know</u> she is in Heaven. She always said that growing up on Morrell Street in the 1930s was heaven for kids, because they had the Rutgers campus right there, and Buccleuch Park, and the river to swim in.

But I think that heaven for her looks a lot like the side yard of 610 Myrtle Road back in the 1970s, when we used to have those big family picnics with everybody there. Billy Ricker and Joey Meyers swapping tall tales, Big Danny McCarthy and Arlene joining right in, Pauline's crazy giggle, the much-missed David Soden and so many of the others who are gone whose names I can't think of at this moment. And you know she's right in the middle of everything, laughing and joking as we speak."

I included the names of people who have already passed because my mother was so family-oriented. Most of my happy memories of her involve gatherings of family and friends at these picnics. I was sure that anyone at the service who had attended those picnics had similar fond memories – and they would all remember my mother being right in the middle of everything, just as I do.

In fact, a cousin who spoke earlier in the service also reminisced about those picnics and how they were some of the best times of his life.

I also included the names of those who had previously passed because I wanted to acknowledge that she was one of the last of her generation to leave us, and that with her passing some of the family history is now gone.

"I want to leave you with some words she wrote in that letter to me about her funeral arrangements.

"Remember me once in awhile. The good things, of course. I wish you all a good life. May you be loved as I loved you all."

As guests arrived at the hall, I greeted them and mentioned that my mother had given me instructions for the memorial service, which is why I said "in that letter."

By ending the eulogy with her words I reinforced the idea that she was a strong person with a positive attitude who cared about others. Her words were meant to comfort, which is why I thought they were the perfect ending to her eulogy.

If there was a particular phrase your loved one used, you may find it helpful to end their eulogy with it. Those gathered will feel they are hearing their loved one for a final time, and it will bring comfort to them.

If not, try to find some words that sum up the departed while offering comfort to those gathered.

CHAPTER FOUR

How to Practice the Eulogy

After you have written the eulogy that you would like to give, practice reading it out loud. Reading it out loud is very important, so don't skip this step.

There are several good reasons for practicing out loud:

1) It will help you clarify what you are trying to say. When you read something out loud, it is easy to spot when sentences are awkward or unclear, or simply don't mean what you want them to mean. Reading it out loud will also enable you to see if you accidentally left something out that you meant to include.

2) You will become aware when your emotions rise and be better able to control them during the service. When I read my mother's eulogy aloud I found myself tearing up when I spoke about her dying peacefully in her sleep. I could not get past the phrase "At least she got that" without having to stop and catch my breath. When I read the words she included in her funeral instructions, especially "may you be loved as I loved you all," I could feel my emotions rise again.

Knowing that these two sections in particular were rough for me to say enabled me to be prepared for my rising emotions when I was speaking at the memorial service, and to make it through without breaking down.

Practice while standing since you probably will be standing when you give the eulogy.

If you can, practice in front of a family member or friend. They will be able to tell you if something is unclear. You may also be able to judge from their reactions while you are reading if there are things that are confusing and whether you are making the impact you intended to.

If your listener starts to get fidgety it may mean that what you have written is too long or too repetitive. Ask your listener to truthfully tell you if it needs to be shorter.

On the other hand, there are people who will insist eulogies have to be at least a certain number of minutes. Ignore them. No one will complain that you didn't speak long enough. Say what you need to say. If that only takes a few minutes, fine. Do not pad the eulogy just to stretch it out. It would be a disservice to your loved one.

Don't feel you have to memorize the whole eulogy word for word. If you feel better doing so, fine. But there is no need for you to put that kind of pressure on yourself. Your emotions on the day will be high, so give yourself a break and refer to your written copy when you need to. People will understand.

Have printed copies of what you are going to say. Make sure you use a large enough font that you will easily be able to refer to your printed copy when you are speaking. Number each page and use a paper clip so you can easily keep the pages in the proper order.

Give one copy to a trusted companion ahead of time in case you lose your copy.

CHAPTER FIVE

How to Handle the Day of the Service

Amemorial service or funeral is very emotional and stressful, therefore you *must* take care of yourself. The last thing your loved one would want is for you to get sick or pass out.

Try to get some rest beforehand. It may be hard but get a full night's sleep if possible, and don't try to do so much before the service that you are exhausted. Conserve your energy for the eulogy.

Stay hydrated.

Try to keep the caffeine to a minimum. If you really feel you need coffee to get through the day, then it is better to have some than go without. However, your nerves will already be on edge, and caffeine could make them worse. Strike a careful balance.

The same with alcohol. Avoid it beforehand if at all possible.

You should wear clothes that you are comfortable in. Appropriate dress, yes, but nothing that is so tight or uncomfortable that it hurts. The same goes for your shoes. Wear ones that are comfortable because you may have to stand for some time, greeting arrivals before the service, speaking at the service, and talking to people afterward. While you may think new shoes would be appropriate, they tend not to be because they aren't broken in.

When delivering the eulogy, try to stand with your feet shoulder-length apart. That's the best position for balance and comfort (not just at the service, but all the time).

Make sure you know the way to the location of the service and get there early. If you believe you will be too upset to drive, enlist a friend or relative who is reliable as your driver. Do not wait until the last minute and then let somebody who doesn't know the way drive you. The person may get lost, and you don't want to worry about getting there on time.

If possible, try to visit the place where the memorial service or funeral is to be held beforehand, especially if you have never been there before. There may be road construction or some other obstacle that could cause a delay, and you will want to build in an extra cushion of time for travel. Also, knowing where to go in the building is one less thing for you to worry about or distract you.

Even if you have been there before, try to visit it again to make sure it's as you remember it.

One way to help calm your nerves before the service is to visit the location beforehand and stand exactly where you will be giving the eulogy. Look at where the service-goers will be sitting, familiarize yourself with the room. If you need to use a podium, now's the time to make sure it is the right height for you.

If there's a microphone, make sure it works.

Make sure there are no lights shining in your eyes. If the lights bother you, ask that they be dimmed ahead of time. If something is distracting, ask for it to be moved.

My mother's service was held in the same hall where food was going to be served buffet style after the eulogy. When I arrived early I saw that the tables where the food was to be laid out were within the view of the people sitting for the service. I was concerned that if the food was put out during the service it would cause a distraction, diverting people's attention and making me uneasy. Before anybody else arrived I had the speaker's stage moved so the food tables were behind where everyone was sitting.

I know these things don't seem important in your time of grief, but making sure everything works ahead of time will enable you to focus on what you are going to say. This process will give you much-needed strength and eliminate the worry about something going wrong while you are speaking.

When it comes time to speak, don't worry if you cry, or need to stop and breathe. Sharing your heart and your love in front of others can be very hard, and you should not be embarrassed or ashamed of doing it.

Also, don't worry if you have to look at your notes or read directly from them. People will understand.

If it gets to be too much just stop, say "excuse me," and look down to compose yourself. Take the time you need, and don't let anyone interrupt you. You'll want to finish the eulogy and you might feel regret if you don't. But if you do feel too overwhelmed, you can ask someone else to read it for you. People will be sympathetic and understand.

CHAPTER SIX

The Main Thing to Remember

The main thing I would like to leave you with is that writing down and sharing your true feelings about your loved one will bring you great comfort. It is a powerful part of the grieving process, and knowing that you captured how you felt about your loss in words will help you in ways that are hard to describe.

When I wrote the eulogy for my mother it brought back many memories, good and bad, and enabled me to see just how much she meant to me, and to see the impact she had on me and those who knew her. In many ways, it brought me closer to her than I had felt in years. Long after the service I am so grateful to reread the memories of her that I put down on paper during the sad days after her passing.

I hope this short manual has helped you put your emotions and memories into words that will bring you comfort in your time of loss. I know this is a hard and difficult time for you, and for many of us writing out our feelings about a loved one is not easy even at the best of times.

I know how difficult it can be. It was hard for me to write about my mother. I became so emotional trying to write down my memories that there were times I had to stop typing and step away from my computer because I was so overcome I could not see the screen clearly. This happened to me despite the fact I have been a professional reporter and writer for more than four *decades*. I can only imagine how tough it would be for people who are not professional writers to find the right words to convey what they are feeling about someone they lost.

If you have tried the steps I described in this manual and are still struggling, I am available to help. I offer personalized services, whether you want help organizing your thoughts and memories, putting your feelings down on paper, or practicing your delivery. Please reach out to me at rulecommunications.com for a free consultation on how I can help you through this tough period.

I leave you with this. Giving a eulogy will help you process your loss. Speaking publicly about your loved one will ease your grief. And in coming days you will be thankful you had the opportunity to give your loved one a proper goodbye. It will bring you solace and comfort as you move forward.

About the Author

B ruce Rule is an award-winning public speaker and veteran journalist with significant experience writing for print, radio and online media. He spent 19 years as an editor at Bloomberg News in New York and London. Prior to Bloomberg, he worked at the Associated Press, Investment Dealers' Digest and the Pottstown Mercury. He also created and published an English-language tourism magazine in Santiago, Chile.

He runs Rule Communications, which provides editing and writing services as well as public speaking coaching for a variety of clients. He lives in Delaware with his wife, Pamela.

Made in the USA
Las Vegas, NV
13 November 2024

11782092R00026